921
OWE

Streissguth, Thomas,
1958-

Jesse Owens.

34880030010511

$25.26

BAKER & TAYLOR

Biography®

Jesse OWENS

Tom Streissguth

A&E®

Lerner Publications Company
Minneapolis

Copyright © 1999 by Lerner Publications Company

Lerner Publications Company
A Division of Lerner Publishing Group
241 First Avenue North
Minneapolis, MN 55401 U.S.A.

Website address: www.lernerbooks.com

Library of Congress Cataloging-in-Publication Data

Streissguth, Thomas, 1958–
    Jesse Owens / Tom Streissguth.
    p.   cm. — (A&E biography)
    Includes bibliographical references and index.
    Summary: Describes the life of the sharecroppers' son who won four gold medals at the 1936 Olympics in Berlin and challenged Hitler's notion of Aryan superiority.
    ISBN 0-8225-4940-9 (alk. paper)
    1. Owens, Jesse, 1913–1980—Juvenile literature. 2. Track and field athletes—United States—Biography—Juvenile literature. [1. Owens, Jesse, 1913– . 2. Track and field athletes. 3. Afro-Americans—Biography.]
I. Title. II. Series.
BF697.O9S87 1999
796.42'092
[b]–DC21   98—30813

Manufactured in the United States of America
1 2 3 4 5 6 – JR – 04 03 02 01 00 99

CONTENTS

Jesse Owens's victories at the 1936 Olympics are memorialized in stone at the entrance to Olympic Stadium in Berlin.

INTRODUCTION

On a rainy afternoon in Berlin, Germany, during early August 1936, Jesse Owens won his first Olympic gold medal by running the 100-meter dash in 10.3 seconds. In the next few days, Owens won three more golds—in the 200-meter dash, in the broad jump, and in the 400-meter relay. He was the first track athlete ever to win four gold medals at a single session of the Summer Olympic Games.

Owens won instant fame and lasting admiration for these athletic feats. But in 1936, his victories meant more than settling the question of who could run the

In the 1930s, many believed that a black person could never be a champion.

The Nazis used these swastika banners as propaganda to sway the minds of many.

fastest or jump the farthest. Owens ran his races in front of Adolf Hitler, the German leader who firmly believed that "Aryans"—an imaginary race of northern Europeans—were superior to all others and especially to African-Americans like Jesse Owens.

Hitler's Nazi Party thrived on symbols. The swastika symbolized Nazi ideas and power. The 1936 Berlin Olympic Games symbolized Germany's revival after a humiliating defeat in World War I. Soldiers marching at the opening ceremonies of the Games symbolized the country's military might. The training and ac-complishments of German athletes symbolized the strength of the German people.

In the days before the August 1 opening ceremony, reporters and spectators arrived from all over the world to watch the "Nazi Olympics." Many of them were impressed with the country's cleanliness, prosperity, and organization. Many greatly admired Germany's ability to stage such an impressive Olympic spectacle. Could any other country in the world have managed it during this time of worldwide economic depression? Some may have thought that these symbols should be taken seriously and that the Nazi belief in racial superiority could be true after all.

Then Jesse Owens, on that rainy August afternoon, took his starting position for a most symbolic event.

A replica of Jesse's Alabama house sits in a park created in his honor.

Chapter **ONE**

ALABAMA BOYHOOD

THE TOWN OF **O**AKVILLE LIES IN NORTH-CENTRAL Alabama in a hilly region known as the Cumberland Plateau. In the early 1900s, Oakville was a farming community, where about a hundred white and black families worked hard to make ends meet on small plots of land. Many of them were sharecroppers who paid rent with the crops they raised, including cotton and corn. The soil was of poor quality, and most Oakville farmers struggled to keep food on their tables and roofs over their heads.

James Cleveland (J. C.) Owens was born in Oakville on September 12, 1913. His first home was a small and drafty wooden house, where he was the last of ten children (three daughters and seven sons) born to

Henry and Mary Emma Owens. After the birth of J. C., the family moved to a slightly larger farm, which they rented from a landowner named James Cannon.

The Owens's new house was hot in summer and drafty in winter. J. C. often came down with colds, as well as bronchitis and pneumonia. He also suffered from painful boils that appeared on his skin. Without money to pay for a doctor's care, his mother would treat the boils herself by cutting them open with a hot kitchen knife.

The Owens family had little money. The floors of their house were bare wooden planks; the children walked them barefoot. But most other families in Oakville were poor as well, and despite his family's poverty, J. C. had a happy boyhood. He was free to play and run in the fields and forests near his house. "I always loved running," he remembered. "I wasn't very good at it, but I loved it because it was something you could do all by yourself, and under your own power. You could go in any direction, fast or slow as you wanted, fighting the wind if you felt like it, seeking out new sights just on the strength of your feet and the courage of your lungs."

Young J. C. wasn't as enthusiastic about school. He paid little attention to his lessons, had trouble learning to read, and skipped school for long periods of time. Each year as the planting and harvest seasons came around, school closed so students could work in the fields. This further hindered his studies.

Life as a sharecropper wasn't much different from slavery. In this picture, a man, instead of a horse, pulls a plow.

No matter how hard the Owenses worked their farm, the family could not get ahead. Every year, they had to give half their crops to the landowner to pay the rent, and they couldn't raise enough money to buy their own land. They were always in debt. Any extra money they had was used to buy clothing and other necessities. J. C.'s clothing was worn and had been frequently mended. His ragged shirts and pants embarrassed him so much that he often hid from neighbor girls to avoid their glances.

Sharecropping was all Henry Owens had ever known. He saw no way out of this life, but J. C.'s mother believed the family could find a better life elsewhere.

Cleveland, like many other large cities, drew sharecroppers away from their farms with the promise of a better life.

She was determined to move away from Oakville some-day, to raise her children under better circumstances and give them a chance at a good education and decent jobs.

Mrs. Owens had heard about the busy factories and large businesses that operated in northern cities such as Detroit and Chicago. These cities were far from Alabama and far from Owens's friends and family. But one of the Owens children, a daughter named Lillie, had moved north to Cleveland, Ohio. Lillie's letters home describing the city convinced Emma Owens that the rest of the family should move. Sometime in the

early 1920s, the Owens family packed up and boarded
a northbound train.

When they arrived in Cleveland, the Owenses moved
into a small apartment on the East Side. They soon
discovered that the neighborhood was full of strangers
like themselves—not only black families from the
South, but also immigrants from Poland, Italy, and
other distant countries. In a busy city like Cleveland,
these families could find work. But the factories,
stores, and construction companies paid low wages.
Like everyone else on the East Side, the Owenses had
to work hard to make ends meet.

Emma Owens and several of her daughters worked
as maids. "My brothers found odd jobs on the same
level," J. C. remembered, "from unloading freight cars

As many as a dozen family members lived in the Owens's duplex house. On the porch sit two sisters, two nieces, his mother, and his brother.

to [working as] part-time janitors. One by one, they had to drop out of school to help bring enough money in for all of us." J. C. was able to stay in school while taking many different part-time jobs—from working in a shoe shop to caring for plants in a greenhouse to delivering groceries.

Although he had already attended school in Oakville, J. C. Owens had to start all over at Bolton Elementary School. He was placed in first grade. The school's principal and teachers were sure that he would have to work hard to catch up with other students his age. But in a short time, J. C. moved up to the second grade. Meanwhile, with the change in surroundings had also come a change in his name. One of his teachers, who couldn't quite make out the young boy's strong Alabama accent, turned "J. C." into "Jesse."

After Bolton, Jesse enrolled at Fairmount Junior High. Like many other city schools, Fairmount emphasized citizenship and work skills as much as academic subjects such as history and math. Although he didn't read well, Jesse advanced with the other students in his class. At Fairmount, Jesse met Minnie Ruth Solomon, who would later become his wife. Ruth had also been born and raised in a southern sharecropper's family and had moved north with her parents.

Fairmount was also where Jesse first took part in organized athletics. Life in the open Alabama air and his love of running had given him speed and stamina; physical education class strengthened his legs and his

Fairmount Junior High School

lungs. Charles Riley, who led the gym class as well as the Fairmount track team, soon introduced himself. "I'd noticed him watching me for a year or so," Jesse recalled. "Especially when we'd play games where there was running or jumping."

Riley saw that Jesse had the potential to do well in track-and-field events such as the high jump and the broad jump (later called the long jump). He encouraged Jesse to train harder than he would for regular gym classes. Since Jesse had to work after school, he agreed to start regular workouts on the running track each morning before school.

Riley carefully coached Jesse on his running style. He taught the boys on his team to run as lightly as possible and to keep their arms, heads, and chests steady while they ran. Jesse's feet, Riley said, must barely touch the ground—as if the track were burning. He must look straight ahead and concentrate on the finish line, not on the other runners. He didn't have to flail about, make faces, or twist his body like a pretzel to get an advantage at the finish line. Riley took Jesse and the other runners to a local racetrack to watch thoroughbred horses run. Like a champion racehorse, Riley pointed out, a good runner makes no unnecessary movements and wastes no energy.

To prepare for competition, Riley had Jesse run distances that were much longer than he would actually have to race. After training for a quarter-mile, he would have an easier time competing in the shorter races such as the 220-yard, 200-yard, and 100-yard dashes (in Europe and in international competition, the standard short sprints were the 100-meter and 200-meter dashes, slightly longer versions of the American sprints).

Jesse was greatly helped by Riley's advice and by a nearly perfect runner's body. He was slender, with strong but not bulky leg muscles. "His proportions were so harmonious," one writer said, "that he did not look outstandingly powerful. When Jesse Owens ran, he never seemed to be desperately pressed. He merely focused on the finish tape and unswervingly, seemingly effortlessly, approached it faster than any competitor did. In movement he was breathtaking to watch. . . . " In every photograph and film of Owens running, he appears to move with ease, while his opponents struggle, turn their heads, and lunge—several feet or yards behind.

Charles Riley also guided Jesse outside of school. The young, promising athlete and the experienced coach became fast friends, sharing meals and spending their spare time together. Riley never said much, and when he spoke, he often talked in riddles.

Jesse's coach, Charles Riley, left, *was like a father to him.*

"Charles Riley was the kind of man who would say something to you when he wanted to, and only then," Jesse later recalled. But Riley's stories and proverbs always carried an important point: winning comes from inner determination and from overcoming the desire to ease off when the going gets hard. As Riley often told Jesse, "Run to beat yourself."

With his hard training and Riley's guidance, Jesse built up the muscles in his legs and developed into the best school athlete in Cleveland. After one year of Riley's coaching, he was clocking just 11 seconds flat in the 100-yard dash, and his marks began showing up in the record books. In 1928, he broke the world junior high school record in the high jump, at 6 feet, and in the broad jump, at 22 feet, 11¾ inches.

That same year, Riley introduced Jesse to Charley Paddock, a world-famous track star. Paddock had just given a talk to the students at Fairmount Junior High. Riley then brought Paddock into his office to meet his most promising young runner. While Jesse listened, Paddock talked about competing in foreign places, such as Antwerp and Paris, where runners from all over the world had raced in the Summer Olympic Games in 1920 and 1924. It may have been the first time Jesse had ever heard about the Olympics. After his meeting with Paddock, Jesse dreamed night and day of making the U.S. Olympic team.

Jesse remained in school, training hard with Charles Riley, while the rest of his family worked. Henry

Edgar Weil, right, *coaches Jesse,* second from right, *and his East Technical High School track teammates.*

Owens and his other sons worked in a Cleveland steel mill. Jesse's sisters continued to work as maids and laundresses. Still, life *was* better in Cleveland than it had been in Oakville. The family had enough food to eat and better clothes to wear.

Emma was sure they had done the right thing by moving north to Cleveland. For Henry Owens, however, one misfortune seemed to follow another. Because he had never learned to read or write, he could find only poor-paying, menial jobs. He may well have felt that he simply didn't belong in the big, noisy northern city. His hair turned gray, and then white. One day in 1929, he was struck by a taxicab and injured. After the accident, he could not find steady work, so he stayed home.

In the fall of 1930, Jesse enrolled at East Technical High School. Students at East Tech prepared for jobs, rather than for college. They could take courses in

The Story of the Olympic Games

Every four years, beginning in 776 B.C., the cities of ancient Greece halted all their battles and sent their best athletes to Olympia. In Olympia, a valley in southwestern Greece, a solemn religious festival was held that included contests of athletic strength and skill. The oldest Olympic event was a footrace that ran the length of the ancient stadium, about two hundred yards. Later Olympic events included boxing, chariot racing, wrestling, discus throwing, and javelin throwing. Winners were awarded laurel wreaths and glory throughout the land. After each victory, the winning athlete was also expected to hold a celebration banquet.

The Olympic Games were so important to the ancient Greeks that they measured their time in "Olympiads." Each Olympiad ran four years, the length of time between sessions of the Games. The first Olympiad began with the first Games in 776 B.C. After Greece was conquered by the Romans, the Games went on, with athletes from foreign countries and Roman colonies all over the Mediterranean region competing. Finally, in A.D. 394, the Roman emperor Theodosius ordered a stop to the Olympic Games. The emperor, a Christian, banned the Games because they were part of a pagan festival. The stadium, practice fields, and temples at Olympia slowly fell into ruin.

In the late 19th century, a French aristocrat named Baron Pierre de Coubertin revived the ancient Games in a modern form. The new Olympics, Coubertin believed, would be a way for the different countries of the world to compete peacefully on the athletic field, rather than violently on the battlefield. Coubertin became president of the International Olympic Committee, and the first modern Olympics were held in Athens, the capital of Greece, in 1896. The first Winter Olympic Games took place in 1924 in Chamonix, France. With few exceptions, the Games have taken place every four years since 1896.

auto mechanics, masonry, and other practical subjects. By 1930, however, Jesse Owens was concentrating on another career: running. Realizing that this
promising athlete needed careful handling, Edgar
Weil, the East Tech track coach, invited Charles Riley
to come to the school in the afternoons and continue
training Jesse.

By then, Jesse was the best-known young track star
in the entire city. By his junior year, he was dominat-
ing every meet he entered and usually scoring more
than half the total points for the East Tech squad. In
the spring of 1932, Jesse's coaches were preparing him
for his biggest challenge yet: a tryout for the U.S.
Olympic team and competition at the Summer
Olympic Games in Los Angeles, California.

Although Jesse was disappointed by his performance at the Olympic tryouts, he proved he was good enough to compete with the best.

Chapter **TWO**

SCHOOLBOY SENSATION

TO CHOOSE THE BEST ATHLETES TO REPRESENT THE
United States in the 1932 Olympics at Los Angeles,
the American Olympic Association held summer tryouts in different regions of the country. That year, the
Midwest tryouts took place at Dyche Stadium at North-
western University in Evanston, Illinois. Jesse Owens
competed in three events: the 100- and 200-meter
dashes and the broad jump. He was already approaching or matching Olympic records in these events. But
under the pressure of competing against the best
athletes in the country, he grew nervous and lost his
concentration. He lost to Ralph Metcalfe, a more experienced runner from Marquette University, and Eddie
Tolan from the University of Michigan.

Jesse was disappointed in his performance at the tryouts, but he began to realize he could compete with the best athletes in the country. He proved it a few weeks later, when an Olympic track squad came to Cleveland for an exhibition event after the close of the Los Angeles Games. This time, Jesse won both the 100- and 200-meter sprints and took second place in the broad jump behind Edward Gordon. As it turned out, Owens had faced the toughest competition in the world that summer. At the Los Angeles Games, Tolan and Metcalfe had finished first and second in the 100-meter dash and placed first and third, respectively, in the 200-meter race. Gordon had won the gold medal in the broad jump.

That same summer, another important event took place in Jesse's life: the birth of his daughter Gloria. Jesse and Ruth had become parents. Although the couple had a child, Ruth continued to live with her father and mother, who helped her take care of the new baby. In his later autobiographies, Jesse Owens claimed to have married Ruth Solomon in secret in Erie, Pennsylvania, because both her parents and his own had opposed the marriage. But some of Jesse's biographers aren't sure. "The marriage license bureau in Erie has no record of any application submitted by James Cleveland Owens or Minnie Ruth Solomon," wrote one biographer. Married or not, Jesse still had a responsibility to help support his daughter and Ruth, who dropped out of school and began to work in a beauty parlor. To earn some needed money, Jesse took a job at a gas station in Cleveland.

Although Jesse struggled to support his young family, his career on the running track was going smoothly. Under Riley's careful coaching, Jesse developed the inner determination and concentration that usually brought him to the finish line first. During his senior year, he won every event he entered and broke several national records. Crowds supported him with boisterous cheering. The track squad elected him captain. His prestige as a track champion also brought his first and last victory as a political candidate. He was elected student council president at East Tech.

Ruth in the hospital with newborn daughter Gloria

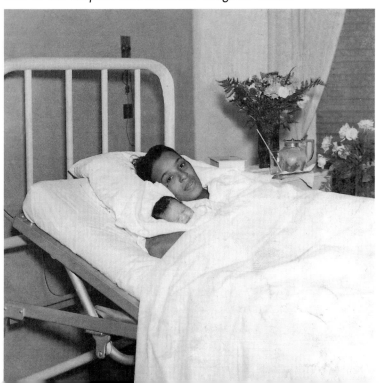

Jesse fills a car with oil at his job as a gas station attendant.

In the spring of 1933, at the Ohio state high school meet, Jesse broke the national high school broad jump record by three inches, jumping 24 feet, 3¾ inches. That June, he competed in the National Interscholastic Championships in Chicago, where he set a new world record of 20.7 seconds in the 220-yard dash. At the same competition, Jesse ran the 100-yard dash in 9.4 seconds, tying a world record, and jumped 24 feet, 9⅝ inches in the broad jump. East Tech easily won the event, with Jesse Owens scoring 30 out of the team's 54 points. Cleveland proudly threw Jesse and the team a victory parade for the big win in Chicago.

In the meantime, Jesse had graduated from high school. He now faced an important decision: where to attend college. Although he always struggled to keep up with his schoolwork, Jesse's great athletic ability brought him the attention of several Big Ten universities. These schools belonged to the biggest and the best athletic conference in the country. Although there were no athletic scholarships available in the 1930s, Jesse and others like him could count on a paying job, arranged by school officials, to help with expenses.

Jesse and Riley drove north to visit the University of Michigan and meet the school's track coaches. The coaches there very much wanted Jesse Owens on their team. Alumni (former students) of the school even offered Henry Owens a job as an apartment caretaker. But Henry was not interested in the job, and a better offer for Jesse soon came from The Ohio State University in the state's capital, Columbus. There Jesse could work part-time as a freight elevator operator in the State House. Although his high school grades were poor, he passed a series of exams that summer that finally qualified him to enter college. He moved to Columbus to start classes in the fall of 1933.

Although Larry Snyder, left, *recognized Jesse's skill as an athlete, he still felt Jesse could improve.*

Chapter **THREE**

COLLEGE BOUND

BECAUSE HE WAS A FRESHMAN, JESSE OWENS was not eligible to be a member of Ohio State's varsity track team. In practices, however, the young coach, Larry Snyder, put Jesse through intensive training sessions. Snyder had Jesse work on the motions of his arms and hands, which Snyder believed were slowing him down. Snyder also had Jesse place his feet closer together at the starting line. The coach believed this new stance would help Jesse react faster to the sound of the starter's gun.

Recognizing Jesse's ability, the Amateur Athletic Union (AAU) awarded him a spot on its All-American team before he had even taken part in a single college track meet. In the spring of 1934, Jesse competed in a national championship meet in New York, organized by the AAU. At this meet, he ran a close second place to Ralph Metcalfe in the 100-meter dash.

Even though he couldn't yet compete for the varsity team in intercollegiate meets, Jesse was permitted to participate in exhibition meets. At one of these exhibitions, the judges let Jesse take a running start before the starting line of a 100-yard dash. He finished the race in just 8.4 seconds, a time that has never been equaled or even approached by any runner with a standing start.

Jesse's new job allowed him plenty of free time to study. He worked only in the evenings, attending to the elevator whenever cleaning crews needed to change floors, about once an hour. While at a desk near the elevator, Jesse tried to keep up with the reading and preparation needed to pass his courses. Nevertheless, he soon fell behind, and by his sophomore year, Jesse was on academic probation, meaning he was in danger of failing Ohio State altogether.

Later that year, Jesse was offered a new job as a page for Ohio's state legislature. When the representatives were called into session to debate and pass laws, he worked as a messenger and office helper in the capitol building. The job as a page carried more prestige than that of a mere elevator operator; Jesse also earned more money.

Jesse finally joined the Ohio State varsity track team in the spring of 1935. Larry Snyder worked with Jesse

Coach Snyder believed Jesse could improve his sprinting time by working on his start.

nearly every day, putting him through thousands of practice starts. Both men knew that the start of any short-distance sprint was crucial. The runner had to get away in a split second and without any hesitation or stumbling. (In later years, sprinters set their feet and pushed off against starting blocks. But in the 1930s, no starting blocks were used. Runners had to dig their feet into the ground and jump at the gun.) Snyder taught Jesse to crouch in a lower and more compact stance in order to get more spring out of his legs at the start.

At his first varsity meet, at the University of Indiana, Jesse won three events. He placed second in his fourth event, the 70-yard low hurdles.

He competed in his first Big Ten finals at Ferry Field in Ann Arbor, Michigan, on May 25, 1935. Before this meet, he had been suffering from a sore back; Coach Snyder nearly benched him. "I'd hurt my back fooling around, wrestling with some friends," Jesse recalled.

"It hurt so much I could barely bend down to start the first event. But once I started to compete, I forgot about it." Jesse astonished his coach and everyone else at the Ann Arbor meet by winning the 220-yard dash in 20.3 seconds; broad-jumping (just once) to a mark of 26 feet, 8¼ inches; and running the 220-yard low hurdles in 22.6 seconds. Each one of these marks was a new world record! His times also represented new world records in the 200-meter dash and 200-meter low hurdles. In the 100-yard dash, Jesse missed another record by just one-tenth of a second, finishing in an official time of 9.4 seconds to tie the world record.

Many sportswriters believe that Jesse's 1935 Ann Arbor meet was the true highlight of his entire athletic career and one of the greatest single showings in track history. After the meet, his teammates elected him captain of the team—the first time an African-American had held the captaincy of any athletic team in the Big Ten. Snyder's coaching and Charles Riley's encouragement had him running at peak form, and he seemed a cinch to make the Olympic team in 1936.

Yet for all his athletic ability and growing fame, Jesse Owens still experienced academic problems, poverty, and racial discrimination. The Ohio State University, like other colleges at the time, had a reputation of not welcoming blacks. While Jesse attended the school, only about a hundred of the fourteen thousand students were African-Americans. Because he was black, Jesse was not allowed to live on campus, where mixing of the races, as well as of men and women, was against the rules. Instead, he had to live in an off-campus boarding-house with other African-American students.

"Many blacks were not permitted in restaurants along High Street," remembered Jesse's teammate Charles Beetham. "They were not permitted in the theaters. In fact about the only place they could eat . . . was in restaurants on the campus." The discrimination was worse when the team traveled. "We had to make arrangements ahead of time for where we would stop to eat," Beetham said. "[Blacks] could not eat in the coffee shop or in the restaurants in the hotel where they stayed. They had to eat in their rooms." Competing in the South, where blacks were strictly banned from any athletic competition with whites, was out of the question.

In the summer of 1935, Jesse and the Ohio State track team toured westward, into California. With all of his success—especially with his world-record per-formances—Jesse had become the track star to see. Newspapers devoted even more attention to his activ-ities, on and off the track. On the track, Jesse won ten events in a row. Off the track, he struck up a friend-ship with a Los Angeles socialite. Photographs showed Jesse and Quincella Nickerson spending time together, and rumors began circulating that they were engaged. When Ruth Solomon heard the rumors, she became angry. She wrote Jesse a letter, then telephoned him. Jesse rushed back to Cleveland, and he and Ruth were

Jesse and Ruth were married at her parents' home in Cleveland.

married the same day he returned home, on July 5, 1935, at the home of Ruth's parents.

Although he was finally a husband, Jesse would have a hard time staying at home. There would be many demands on his time. But Jesse was restless by nature, and the constant travel and a busy calendar suited him well. On top of it all, the Olympic Games were fast approaching, and he was already favored to bring home some gold medals. But he was still too inexperienced to worry about how his schedule would affect Ruth and Gloria, or what the future would bring to a promising athlete who excelled in a strictly amateur sport.

That summer, Jesse won a position as an honorary page for a legislative committee. Since the legislature did not meet in the summer, he did not have any specific duties. Instead he was free to train, travel, and compete with the help of the twenty-one dollars a week the appointment paid him. For several weeks that summer, Jesse collected and spent money from the state government while never setting foot in the state capitol.

Certainly the money and the free time helped him. But his position as an honorary page also nearly kept him from participating in the 1936 Olympics. The Amateur Athletic Union had a large representation on the American Olympic Association, and its rules were very strict. AAU athletes could not earn money for taking part in athletic competition. Nor could they benefit through awards, prizes, or political appointments and jobs. To AAU officials, Jesse seemed to be profiting from his ability on the running track, not from his qualifications as a page. The $159 he had earned from a no-show job looked suspiciously like an illegal athletic scholarship. In August 1935, the AAU decided to investigate.

Jesse had to appear in Cleveland and explain his appointment. Many of the officials who listened to his story were sympathetic. His family had no money to support him, and he needed as much time as possible to remain in shape for competition. Persuaded by Ohio State officials who testified for their star runner, the Northeastern Ohio AAU Eligibility Committee decided in his favor, and that fall, Jesse decided to return the money he had earned as an honorary page.

To make matters worse, Jesse was suspended from the track team because of his poor grades and had to practice on his own. But the suspension did not discourage him in the least. Although it had been a full three years since his last attempt to make the Olympic team, this time he was faster, better trained, and more confident. Jesse knew the 1936 Olympics, if he should make the team, might be his best chance ever to place himself among the world's best runners and athletes.

Jesse didn't yet realize there would be much more to the 1936 Games than track and field and other athletic events. Back in the spring of 1932, the International Olympic Committee had decided to hold the 1936 Olympic Games in Germany. The Winter Games would take place in Garmisch-Partenkirchen, a ski resort in the Alps of southern Germany. The Summer Games would take place in the German capital of Berlin.

Since taking power in 1933, Germany's Nazi Party had been preparing for the 1936 Olympic Games. The Nazi leader, Adolf Hitler, saw the Games as an opportunity to show the world that Nazi economic and social policies were a success. He also saw the Games as an opportunity for German athletes to prove his theories about the superiority of "Aryan" people.

Life in Nazi Germany

fter Adolf Hitler's National Socialist (Nazi) Party won Germany's elections in early 1933, the country swiftly became a one-party dictatorship. The Nazi Party took control of the economy, education, the press, and nearly every aspect of Germany's cultural life, including organized athletics. Those who disagreed with Hitler's words or deeds found themselves quickly out of favor, out of their jobs, imprisoned, or in exile in another country.

Hitler based many of his ideas and actions on the theory that Germans and other Caucasian people of northern Europe were physically and mentally superior to other races around the world. According to him, the Germans had been defeated in World War I not on the battlefield but through the treachery of certain people within Germany, particularly Jews. After taking power, the Nazis forced many German Jews and other "non-Aryans" out of their jobs and their homes. Jews began leaving the country by the thousands, while many who stayed were imprisoned simply because of their heritage and religion. Hitler made it clear that he was determined to exterminate all Jews.

Nazi policies even affected those who were promoting Germany's effort to host the Olympic Games. Theodor Lewald, the president of the German Olympic Committee, was nearly thrown out of the organization—not because he was Jewish, but because he had a Jewish ancestor. Lewald had led the drive to bring the Olympic Games to Berlin, but the success of his efforts had counted for nothing in the eyes of the Nazi leadership. In Lewald's defense, the International Olympic Committee threatened to move the Games to another country if he was removed. The Nazis allowed Lewald to remain but limited his decision-making authority to almost nothing.

Jesse Owens may not have given Adolf Hitler or the Nazi Party much thought as he prepared to qualify for the U.S. Olympic team. But many other people were giving Hitler attention, and many firmly believed that the United States should boycott (refuse to attend) the 1936 Games to protest Hitler's racist and anti-Jewish policies and actions. Jewish athletes were banned from Germany's amateur sporting clubs, whose members were the only athletes allowed to try out for the Olympic team. Jews could not participate in any organized team sport. They could not work out in the gyms, practice in swimming pools, or join equestrian or fencing clubs.

Former Olympian Avery Brundage, the president of the American Olympic Association, supported the idea of a U.S. boycott. But others opposed it, believing that racial discrimination was just as bad in the United States as it was in Germany. They saw no reason to deprive young athletes of the chance to disprove Hitler's racist theories at the Games. Some opposed the boycott on the grounds that the United States shouldn't meddle in Germany's affairs. A few believed that Germany didn't discriminate at all. Frederick W. Rubien, the secretary of the American Olympic Association, said that "Germans are not discriminating against Jews in their Olympic tryouts. The Jews are eliminated because they are not good enough as athletes. Why, there are not a dozen Jews in the world of Olympic calibre."

After Germany announced that a group of German Jewish athletes would be allowed to take part in Olympic training, Brundage decided to go to Germany and judge the conditions for himself. Brundage toured the country as well as the Olympic facilities under construction in Berlin, and met with several German Jewish leaders (always accompanied by Nazi officials). He was impressed by the country's prosperity and orderliness, and was convinced by the arguments of German leaders that their anti-Jewish policies had changed. In fact, Germany *had* allowed hockey player Rudi Ball and fencer Helene Mayer, both of whom were German Jews in exile, to return to Germany to participate on Olympic teams.

After his tour, Brundage decided that Hitler's regime was following the Olympic rules of fair play and amateurism. When he returned to the United States, he recommended that the country send a team. Conditions seemed to be improving, and, he argued, the actions of a single nation did not justify threatening the international Olympic program through a boycott. In late 1935, the AAU also changed its mind and withdrew from the boycott. In the meantime, under the Nuremberg Laws passed in Germany in September 1935, Jewish athletes and ordinary Jewish citizens had been stripped of their citizenship and of their right to protection under German laws.

Amid all the controversy, Jesse kept running, jumping, and winning. "I wanted no part of politics," he wrote later. "The purpose of the Olympics, anyway, was to do your best." His grades had improved, and in the spring of 1936 he was allowed to rejoin the Ohio State track team and take part in Big Ten competition. On May 16, 1936, at the University of Wisconsin at Madison, he set a new world record in the 100-yard dash with a time of 9.3 seconds. At the Big Ten championships held a week later on his home track at Ohio State, Jesse won all four events he entered. That spring he was running at peak form, and word of his ability quickly spread overseas. Fans and sportswriters were looking forward to seeing what Jesse could do in Berlin.

Eulace Peacock and Ralph Metcalfe were Jesse's toughest competition at the Olympic trials. Peacock had also been born in Alabama and was a year younger than Jesse. A football and track star from Temple University, he was larger and stronger than Jesse. In sprints and broad jump competition, the two made nearly identical marks. The summer before, Peacock was also in top form and had beaten Jesse five straight times in just a few days.

Ralph Metcalfe already held three Olympic medals from the 1932 Games in Los Angeles. "Ralph was tall, yet powerful," Jesse wrote, "with legs longer and more heavily muscled than mine, a chest with more lung capacity." At the Olympic tryout finals, held at Randall's Island in New York on July 11 and 12, Owens and Metcalfe easily made the team. Jesse

After earning back his spot on the Ohio State track team, Jesse, second runner from left, **won race after race.**

won all three of his events: the 100-meter and 200-meter dashes as well as the broad jump. David Albritton, a friend of Jesse's from East Technical High School and Ohio State, also qualified to compete in the high jump. But Eulace Peacock suffered a hamstring injury and did not make the team.

Owens and Metcalfe were two of nineteen African-American athletes to qualify for the 1936 U.S. Olympic team. Ten were on the men's track team; two were on the women's track squad. Other African-Americans were on the boxing and weightlifting teams. Jesse and his teammates would take center stage in Berlin at an Olympics hosted by a nation that, under Hitler's influence, was coming to believe in its own racial superiority. All the world would be watching.

This runner is the last of the three thousand runners who relayed the Olympic flame from Olympia, Greece, to Berlin for the 1936 Games.

Chapter **FOUR**

BERLIN

IT WAS NOT EASY TO SELECT, PREPARE, TRANSPORT, and provide for a 382-member Olympic team, especially during the Great Depression. The amateur tradition of the modern Games made the tasks even more difficult. By Baron Pierre de Coubertin's strict standards, Olympic athletes could not earn money from athletic contests of any kind. The AAU, the American Olympic Association, and Avery Brundage himself watched very carefully over the activities of Olympic athletes to make sure they did not break, or even bend, the rules.

To pay expenses for the U.S. team, the American Olympic Association asked for donations from groups such as the AAU and the National Collegiate Athletic

Association (NCAA). In turn, the NCAA asked its member schools to contribute funds. But contributions from several universities, including Ohio State, came slowly and amounted to less than expected. To make sure the team's bills would be paid, the AAU scheduled a series of track-and-field exhibition meets to take place in Europe just after the close of the Olympic Games. Confident that the U.S. team would do well in Berlin, the AAU figured on drawing large crowds to see Jesse Owens and his teammates perform.

Jesse probably did not give the post-Olympic exhibitions much thought as he and the rest of the team boarded the passenger liner SS *Manhattan* on July 15, 1936, for the voyage to Europe. Larry Snyder also took the trip, although he had to pay his own way. The trip lasted nine days through rough seas and stormy weather. While Jesse and several other members of the team struggled with seasickness, a few athletes made the mistake of simply eating too much. With nowhere to train or work off their meals, they found themselves a few pounds heavier and out of shape by the time the ship docked in Europe.

For the most part, Jesse enjoyed the voyage; it was the first time he had ever been on a ship. His easygoing manner had a way of attracting strangers, and he found himself signing hundreds of autographs for fans as well as teammates. At the end of the voyage, the rest of the team voted him the best-dressed athlete,

Some of Jesse's teammates aboard the SS Manhattan, from left to right: *Jimmy LuValle, Archie Williams, John Woodruff, Ben Johnson, Matthew Robinson.*

and he came in second in the vote for most popular athlete, behind distance runner Glenn Cunningham.

On July 24, 1936, the *Manhattan* finally called at the German port of Bremerhaven. After reaching Berlin by express train, the U.S. athletes, with athletes from fifty-one other countries, were given a tour of the elaborate facilities prepared by Germany for the Games. The largest of the nine arenas was the gigantic Olympic Stadium, which could hold 110,000 spectators.

Hitler had closely supervised Germany's preparations for the Games. His orders were to put the nation's best foot forward—there must be no visible discrimination against Jews, and arrests of German residents opposed to Nazism should temporarily stop. "He gave orders that everything should be done to convey the impression of a peace-minded Germany to the many prominent foreign guests," wrote Albert Speer, who worked at Hitler's side as his personal architect.

German companies had devised and built advanced measuring devices to be used for the first time at the Berlin Games. Olympic judges could make use of a new high-speed camera for the finishes of swimming and track races, an electronic scoreboard, and a sensing device to detect the touches made on opponents by fencers with their épées (fencing swords). The Berlin Games were also the first to be televised, using a small local network of receivers stationed around the German capital.

The opening ceremonies for the 1936 Summer Olympic Games took place on Saturday, August 1. Thousands of soldiers, schoolchildren, and bands marched through the streets and into the stadium in close formation. At 3 P.M., Hitler arrived. He was described by the American writer Thomas Wolfe as "a little dark man with a comic-opera mustache, erect and standing, moveless and unsmiling, with his hand upraised, palm outward. . . ." The Olympic pyre was lit by a flaming torch, which—for the first time—had been relayed from the ruins of Olympia in Greece. More than three thousand runners had carried their torches in turn to bring the flame from Olympia to the opening ceremonies in Berlin. The national teams marched solemnly around the track, each holding their nation's flag in the front rank.

Sunday, August 2, was the first day of competition. In the morning, a member of the German team, Hans Woellke, won the shot-put competition with a throw

Creating an Olympic Village

In preparation for the 1936 Games, German architects had designed the biggest and best housing and training facilities ever seen for athletes. An Olympic Village, the first of its kind, was built a few miles west of Berlin. The village had 160 separate cottages, each of which housed twenty-four male athletes. (Women were housed in a large dormitory building.) Natural and artificial lakes stocked with fish and tame ducks dotted the grounds. Athletes could enjoy a library, a theater, practice fields, and a swimming pool. Doctors, dentists, barbers, and masseuses were available, and a guide who spoke the team's language lived in each cottage.

Meals were selected to suit the taste of each national team. Bed mattresses with the proper firmness or softness were installed. German officials also had devised a very thorough system of color-coded papers that told the athletes where they were to stay, where and when they would eat, and when buses would take them to the correct stadium or complex for their events. The Berlin Olympic Village served as a model for the villages that would be built for Olympic athletes after World War II.

of 53 feet, 1¾ inches. Woellke was the first German
competitor to win any track-and-field event in the
modern Olympic Games. After the victory ceremony,
Hitler invited Woellke to come to the official presidential box and receive a handshake and personal
congratulations on the victory. Later, three Finnish
athletes took first, second, and third place in the
10,000-meter run, while German women took gold
and silver medals in the javelin throw. All received
Hitler's personal congratulations.

The main event of the first day was the high jump.
Cornelius Johnson of the United States won the event
with a jump of 7 feet, 6¼ inches. But Hitler left his
observation box and the stadium without congratulat-
ing or meeting Johnson, an African-American. After
meeting the other athletes, Hitler had been warned by
the president of the International Olympic Committee,
Henri Baillet-Latour, that he must not show any fa-
voritism—either all gold medalists should receive his
congratulations, or none should. Hitler decided none
would. His hasty exit before Johnson's win in the high
jump was later understood by many writers to have
been a snub of Jesse Owens as well.

On the same day, Jesse was scheduled to compete in
the preliminary heats for the 100-meter dash. There
were twelve elimination heats for the field of sixty-
eight entrants, then a series of four quarterfinals and
semifinals. In the last preliminary race, Jesse ran the
sprint in 10.3 seconds, tying the Olympic record. In

the quarterfinals, held that afternoon, he ran the race in 10.2 seconds. But his time did not go into the record books. A strong wind blowing at the runners' backs that afternoon helped their sprints and disqualified Jesse's extraordinary time.

The 100-meter finals took place the next day, on August 3. A storm had passed earlier in the day, and the inside track—Jesse's lane—was soft and muddy. Before starting the race, the judges moved the entire field one lane to the right so the soft conditions would not put any runner at a disadvantage.

Jesse took his starting position alongside Ralph Metcalfe and Frank Wykoff of the United States, Erich Borchmeyer of Germany, Lennart Strandberg of Sweden, and Martinus Osendarp of the Netherlands. The starter raised his gun. The audience waited, expecting a spectacular race and perhaps even a new record. "I was looking only at the finish line and realizing that five of the world's fastest humans wanted to beat me to it . . . ," Jesse later said.

When the gun sounded, Jesse took the lead immediately, while Metcalfe in the outside lane stumbled and fell behind the pack. Then Metcalfe began passing the others. As the runners approached the tape, Metcalfe passed Osendarp and gained on Jesse. At the finish line, Jesse was still about a meter in front of Metcalfe. Osendarp came in third, Wykoff fourth, Borchmeyer fifth, and Strandberg last. The winning time was 10.3 seconds, again tying the Olympic record.

More than a hundred thousand people rose to their feet, cheering as Jesse Owens jogged around the track for a victory lap. As Hitler watched and listened, the crowd chanted Jesse's name. Jesse had won his first Olympic gold medal and, in just 10.3 seconds, had become the star of the 1936 Olympic Games.

The next day, Jesse ran in the preliminaries for the 200-meter dash. There would be two preliminary races to decide the runners in the semifinal races to be held on August 5. The track had dried out, helping Jesse to run both races in 21.1 seconds, a new world record for 200-meter races held on a curved track.

That afternoon, the broad jump preliminaries took place. Jesse was favored to win the event—after all, he

Judges, lower left, *mark finish times as Jesse,* upper right, *wins his first gold medal.*

already held the world record of 26 feet, 8¼ inches. But he first needed to qualify for the finals with a jump of at least 23 feet, 5½ inches. Jesse expected to have no problem since he had been passing that mark since high school.

Still wearing his sweat suit, Jesse began limbering up on the inside field. He jogged along the track to get the feel of the ground and the takeoff board, then took a short practice run through the pit. Suddenly, a red flag went up. His practice run had been counted as one of his three tries by the judges! In his first official Olympic broad jump, Jesse Owens had not even left the ground.

On the second try, Jesse made sure to take a jump. But he allowed his foot to touch beyond the front edge of the takeoff board. The judges raised the disqualification flag once again. Jesse had only one try left to qualify for the broad jump finals. This time, he gave himself plenty of room behind the takeoff board, planted his foot solidly, and jumped just one-half inch past the qualifying mark.

Sixteen athletes took part in the finals of the broad jump competition. Jesse was the favorite. His strongest competition came from a German athlete named Luz Long. To many onlookers, the head-to-head competition between Jesse and Long seemed to represent a test of the Nazi theories of racial superiority. Long was tall and blond, a perfect model for Hitler's "Aryan" type, while Jesse was black. The Nazis considered

Jesse not only won a gold medal for this broad jump at the Berlin Olympics, he also set a world record.

blacks "primitive" and "subhuman." Jesse himself remembered that "Long was one of those rare athletic happenings, a perfectly proportioned body . . . stunningly compressed and honed by tens of thousands of obvious hours of sweat and determination."

The two men jumped nearly equal marks in the first try of the finals. On the second, Owens jumped just over 26 feet, the first time in history that an Olympic athlete had gone 26 feet in the broad jump. The two athletes continued, nearly matching each other through several more tries. In all, Long and Owens tied the Olympic record once and beat it five times. On his last jump, Jesse leaped an amazing 26 feet, 5⁵⁄₁₆

Luz Long's broad jump was good but not good enough to beat Jesse.

inches, establishing the new Olympic record. "I decided I wasn't going to come down," Jesse remembered. "I was going to stay up in the air forever."

Long had fouled on his next-to-last jump, and then could only make 25 feet, 9¾ inches—still better than the old Olympic record. Although he had lost, Long rushed up to Jesse and immediately congratulated his opponent on the victory. The two men walked off the field together, and from that moment on they remained friends.

The rainy weather continued as Jesse prepared for his last event: the 200-meter finals. He had easily qualified and then won his semifinal heat with a time of 21.3 seconds, just one-tenth of a second slower than the Olympic record. But Jesse knew he would probably have to do better than that to beat his main competition: his own teammate Mack Robinson, the elder brother of a rising young athletic star named Jackie Robinson.

The finals took place on August 5. The competitors were Owens, Robinson, Martinus Osendarp and Wijnand van Beveren of the Netherlands, Paul Hänni of Switzerland, and Lee Orr of Canada. But from the instant the starting gun sounded, Jesse Owens ran well ahead of the field. He crossed the finish line three meters ahead of Robinson and Osendarp, shattering the old Olympic and curved track world records with a time of 20.7 seconds. It was Jesse's third gold medal.

Jesse hoped to spend the rest of the Olympic Games resting, watching, and signing autographs. But to his surprise, he was entered in one more race. On August 7, the coach of the 400-meter relay team, Dean Cromwell, picked Jesse and Ralph Metcalfe to run in place of Sam Stoller and Marty Glickman.

Stoller and Glickman happened to be the only two Jewish athletes on the U.S. track-and-field team. They had come to Berlin to compete and to show up Hitler, whose opinion of Jews, by this time, was well known to them and to the rest of the world. Now Cromwell had suddenly changed the lineup to Owens, Foy Draper, Frank Wykoff, and Ralph Metcalfe. Stoller and Glickman were off the relay team.

The decision stunned every member of the team. Glickman reacted angrily, pointing out that the substitutions were unnecessary—any four runners from the team would probably win the relay. Jesse's reaction to the decision, as Marty Glickman later remembered, was to protest. "Coach, let Marty and Sam run," Jesse said. "I've had enough. I've won three gold medals. Let them run. They deserve it." The coach told Jesse to run anyway.

Writers and athletes still argue over Cromwell's reasons for dropping Stoller and Glickman from the relay team. Cromwell may have believed, as he told the team, that the Germans had saved their best runners for the race and that adding Owens and Metcalfe gave his squad its best chance of winning. Others believe Dean Cromwell wanted Draper and Wykoff on the team because the two runners attended the University of Southern California, where Cromwell coached. Glickman believed Cromwell simply acted out of anti-Semitism, and that the coach wanted to save Adolf Hitler the embarrassment of seeing his team beaten by a squad that included Jewish runners.

On the morning of August 8, during a trial heat, the new U.S. relay team ran the semifinal race in 40 seconds, equaling the world-record time. That afternoon, in the finals, Jesse Owens ran the first leg and gave the team a lead of five meters. At the end of a hundred meters, he passed the baton to Ralph Metcalfe, who gunned out well in front of the field and added two

meters to the lead. Draper and Wykoff finished the relay
with the U.S. team fifteen meters ahead of second-
place Italy. The squad had set a new world record
time of 39.8 seconds—a mark that would stand for
twenty years.

Jesse Owens carried away four gold medals, three
more than any other track athlete in Berlin and more
than anyone else to that point in Olympic track his-

Although not originally a member, Jesse helped the U. S. relay team win a gold medal and break records.

tory. He also set three new world records. Although Germany won the overall competition, with a total of thirty-three gold medals, the United States had finished in second place overall and had dominated the track-and-field events. Also, with the entire world watching, Jesse Owens's performance had shown Hitler's theories on race to be nonsense. "[Hitler] followed the athletic contests with great excitement," wrote Albert Speer. "Each of the German victories—and there were a surprising number of these—made him happy, but he was highly annoyed by the series of triumphs by the marvelous colored American runner, Jesse Owens. People whose antecedents came from the jungle were primitive, Hitler said with a shrug; their physiques were stronger than those of civilized whites. They represented unfair competition and hence must be excluded from future games."

In fact, there would be no athletes competing at all in the next two Olympic years, 1940 and 1944. Because of the war Hitler would launch against Poland and the rest of Europe in 1939, the Olympic Games would, in time, be canceled twice. Not until 1948 were the summer contests held again. In ancient Greece, war stopped with each Olympics. In modern times, the Olympic Games were stopped for war.

Jesse celebrates his Olympic victories, wearing his laurel leaves and holding three of his medals.

Chapter FIVE

GOING HOME

JESSE OWENS WAS PACKING HIS BAGS, SIGNING autographs, posing for photographs, and preparing for the voyage home. He had nearly forgotten that the U.S. track team still had work to do. The AAU had committed the team to several exhibition meets that were to start before the end of the Berlin Games. Even though the American Olympic Association had eventually raised enough money to cover the expenses of competing in the 1936 Games, the AAU intended to honor its contracts for the exhibitions. Jesse and the other athletes would earn nothing, ensuring that their amateur standing would not be jeopardized.

So, instead of taking a restful voyage back across the Atlantic Ocean, Jesse had to board planes and trains

British boys run with Jesse during a workout.

for shorter trips across Europe. The first stop was Cologne, in western Germany, where Ralph Metcalfe edged out Jesse in the 100-meter dash. The next day, the team boarded an early morning flight for Prague, Czechoslovakia. Jesse ran that evening, then boarded another train for Bochum, Germany, where he would compete the following day. The day after that, he was in London, preparing for more sprints, broad jumps, photographs, interviews, autographs, and admiring crowds.

The tough competition at the Olympics had already drained Jesse physically. He couldn't hope to match the marks he had made in Berlin. His family was back home, and he was receiving numerous job offers, some that would pay well, for his era. Still broke and often hungry, Jesse had trouble concentrating on his events and felt a growing resentment at being put on show like a prize-winning horse.

After reaching London, Jesse competed in a 400-meter relay race. Then, at a press conference, he declared, "I'm burned out, I'm busted, and I'm tired of being treated like cattle. I know how hard it is for a member of my race to make money... and I have to reach for it while it's being offered me."

Eager to get home and explore job opportunities, Jesse cuts short his European tour.

Jesse had a long talk with Larry Snyder. Following Snyder's advice and encouragement, Owens deliberately missed the plane to Sweden. While the rest of the team continued on to Scandinavia and more exhibitions, Owens and Snyder boarded the passenger ship *Queen Mary* and returned to the United States.

Skipping the rest of the tour turned out to be one of the most important decisions of Jesse Owens's life. The leaders of the AAU were outraged. Even though Jesse had earned nothing from the Olympics or from the exhibitions, the AAU announced that Jesse would be suspended immediately and indefinitely. He would be barred from competing in AAU-sponsored events in the United States.

The suspension may have worried Jesse, but he had other things to think over on the return voyage to New York. He had already received offers from agents and stars in Hollywood and New York. Eddie Cantor, a radio and stage comedian, had made an offer of $40,000 for Jesse to appear in a series of vaudeville broadcasts. On top of all that, Ohio State wanted Jesse to return and finish his college education, as he was sure to be a big draw at the school's upcoming track meets.

Cleveland, meanwhile, had prepared a welcoming party to meet Jesse's train from New York. The city put on a victory parade and a grand celebration in front of City Hall, where the mayor and other officials delivered speeches of praise. Another parade wound

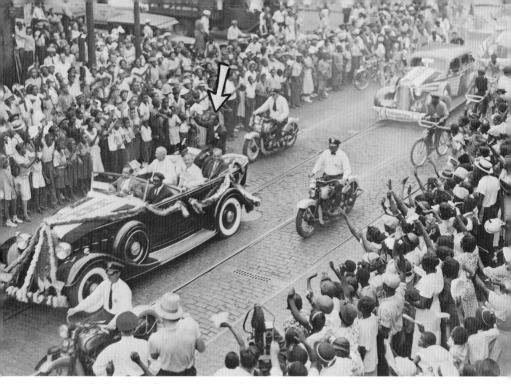

Hailed as the fastest man in the world, Jesse received many ticker tape parades.

through the streets of Columbus, where the mayor and the Ohio governor personally greeted the world's fastest man. When the other members of the track team arrived from Europe, Jesse returned to New York City to ride in the front car of a motorcade and to attend a medal ceremony hosted by New York's mayor, Fiorello La Guardia.

At the same time, Jesse had to think carefully about his future. A college degree would give him further prestige and help him land a good-paying job. (In fact, Wilberforce University in Wilberforce, Ohio, was already offering him a job as its track coach—provided he obtained his degree.) On the other hand, he might never again have a chance to use his worldwide fame, which could be gone in a very short time. So Jesse decided to quit college, for the time being, and take advantage of the offers that were coming his way.

In New York, Jesse signed a contract with a professional agent named Marty Forkins. Forkins would screen all the offers and negotiate contracts. Jesse had been introduced to Forkins by Bill "Bojangles" Robinson, a famous dancer and movie star. Several large companies had already hired Jesse to promote their products in print and on the radio. Jesse also accepted paid offers to make personal appearances and speak at public events.

Politicians also saw an appearance by Jesse Owens, the best-known athlete in the world, as a helpful part of their campaigns. Presidential elections were the Olympic Games of U.S. politics, and like the Olympic Games, they came around every four years. For the election of 1936, both the Democratic and Republican parties wanted to use Jesse Owens's famous name and build on his public support.

Politicians had never paid much attention to athletes, especially to African-American athletes. By 1936 things were beginning to change. For many years, African-American voters had remained loyal to the Republican Party, the party of Abraham Lincoln. During the Great Depression, President Franklin Roosevelt and the Democratic Party had made laws that had helped unemployed, hungry, and desperate families, black as well as white. Roosevelt was popular all over the country, and many people believed black voters for the first time would vote Democratic. For either party, Jesse Owens would be useful in helping black voters make up their minds.

Jesse thought things over and decided to support the Republican candidate, Alf Landon. He was paid generously by Republican Party backers for his endorsement, although nobody is sure how much money changed hands. In September and October of 1936, Jesse traveled all over the East and Midwest to talk about the Berlin Olympic Games and the U.S. presidential election. But in politics, Jesse didn't run quite as well as he did in the Olympics. The forty-eight states, including a solid majority of African-American voters, sided with Franklin Roosevelt, who beat Landon in a November election landslide.

Jesse Owens may have barely noticed Landon's defeat, since his life had grown increasingly busy. Solitary training on the running track had given way to a life of crowds, appointments, speeches, interviews, travel, and deals. In a strange way, however, going everywhere at once helped him get nowhere in particular. Despite his victories and fame, Jesse still had no permanent job, and he soon found himself struggling to give his life some direction.

Jesse didn't see much of his wife, Ruth, while he was campaigning and making endorsements.

Chapter **SIX**

RUNNING FOR MONEY

WHILE JESSE OWENS CAMPAIGNED WITH ALF LANDON and the Republican Party, Marty Forkins was making hundreds of telephone calls from his office in New York City on behalf of Jesse. He arranged for Jesse to endorse products in newspapers and on the radio and to give speeches at ball games and banquets. Forkins talked with movie producers about landing Jesse a starring role in a Hollywood film. But the offers from Hollywood, and even the $40,000 offer from Eddie Cantor, all turned out to be nothing more than empty promises.

Jesse paid little heed. His appearances and endorsements were earning him more than he could have dreamed of earning before the Olympics. He bought a new car and a new house. He bought a fine house for his struggling parents. He bought new clothes for himself and jewelry for Ruth. He made a down payment on a new car for Charles Riley, the junior high track coach who had done so much to prepare him for competition.

Banned from amateur track meets, Jesse became a one-man running exhibition. It was the only way for him to profit as an athlete—after all, there were no professional track teams or broad-jumping leagues. The exhibitions were partly an athletic event and partly a circus spectacle. Most took place before baseball games. Jesse was pitted against the fastest members of the hometown team for a sprint down the first-base line. He also broad jumped and raced over low hurdles, sometimes giving his competitors a head start of ten or twenty yards. At one exhibition in Chicago, he raced against heavyweight boxer Joe Louis.

One famous stunt arranged by his agent took place during the halftime of a soccer match in Havana, Cuba, in late 1936. Jesse had been scheduled to race against Cuba's fastest human, Conrado Rodrigues. But after the AAU threatened to revoke Rodrigues's amateur standing in the United States, the Cuban sprinter backed out. Marty Forkins then arranged for Jesse Owens to run against a thoroughbred racehorse named Julio McCaw. Because Jesse had a forty-yard head start, he beat the horse by a few yards and earned $2,000.

Jesse had not planned to race against a horse.

While appearances and exhibition events earned Jesse money and some comfort, they also earned him scorn from some writers and officials involved in amateur sports. Many of them disliked Jesse's eagerness to profit from his success at Berlin. The members of the Sullivan Committee, who made an annual award to the year's best amateur athlete, snubbed Jesse by voting him second place in 1936. Despite Jesse's record-setting performances in Berlin, the recipient of the

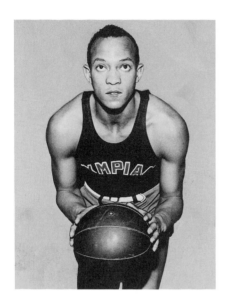

Jesse coached the Olympians professional basketball teams for less than a year because the AAU would not allow amateur teams to play against them.

Sullivan Trophy that year was Glenn Morris, winner of the Olympic decathlon (ten-event competition).

New athletic stars were coming along, and appearance offers for Jesse began to slow. In the winter of 1936–1937, Jesse Owens was looking for a more permanent engagement. In January 1937, Consolidated Radio Artists hired him to lead a twelve-piece dance band on a coast-to-coast tour. Jesse's job was to stand up in front of the band and announce each number. "They had me sing a little," Jesse recalled, "but that was a horrible mistake. I can't carry a tune in a bucket." The job itself was easy enough, but the constant travel soon began to wear on Jesse's nerves and on his health.

In April 1937, Jesse quit the band. That fall, he started a professional basketball squad that he named the Olympians. The team traveled from city to city, playing against local amateur clubs as well as college teams. At halftime, Owens gave short talks and put on demonstrations of his running skill and speed. The team earned money and won most of its games, but it soon ran into trouble with the AAU. According to AAU rules, any team that participated in amateur events could not profit from its touring; it could only make

Jesse, kneeling, ***poses with an Olympians basketball team.***

Jesse only worked his dry-cleaning business for a few months before running into money problems.

enough money to pay expenses. The AAU barred college squads from playing against the Olympians, and in the spring of 1938, the squad was disbanded.

Jesse Owens decided to settle down in Cleveland with his family, which had grown to include another daughter, Marlene. In the summer of 1938, he took a job as a playground director. That fall he started a dry-cleaning business with two partners. But Jesse took little interest in the day-to-day details of running the Jesse Owens Dry Cleaning Company. In the fall and winter of 1938–1939, the company struggled to meet its many debts on loans and equipment.

In 1939 the Jesse Owens Dry Cleaning Company closed down, and Jesse himself filed for bankruptcy. After all the exhibitions and personal appearances and the touring and speaking fees he had earned, he had only $2,050 in assets, and debts of $8,891. He also owed money to the Internal Revenue Service, or IRS (the government's tax-collection agency). The IRS discovered that Jesse had failed to pay income tax on $20,000 he had earned after the Berlin Olympics. Jesse asked a court to protect him from the many creditors who had lent him money. He would spend many years paying it all back.

After settling his bankruptcy case in Cleveland, Jesse Owens went back on the road to tour and earn money. In 1939 he traveled with the Indianapolis Clowns and the Toledo Crawfords, baseball teams that played in the Midwest and the South. At the end of each game, Jesse would don a track suit and race against the fastest man in town, giving his opponent a ten-yard lead and always winning. He also kept racing against horses. Many years later, the memory left him sad and bitter. "I was no longer a proud man who had won four Olympic gold medals," he wrote. "I was a spectacle, a freak who made his living by competing—dishonestly—against dumb animals. I hated it. . . ."

Although the money Jesse was earning helped him begin to pay off his many debts, he still sensed that he was getting nowhere fast. Jesse had lost control of his life and was drifting aimlessly from one playing field to another. He also experienced problems and tragedies in his personal life. His long absences from home often left his wife alone to care for their daughters. Then in March 1940, Jesse's mother died.

Spectators who watched Jesse run were beginning to forget about his accomplishments in the Olympic Games. His name had disappeared from the sports pages. By 1940, sports fans and sportswriters were beginning to look around for another candidate as the "World's Fastest Human." Other athletes were approaching and sometimes beating some of Jesse's world and national records in sprints and hurdles.

Jesse decided that better-paying exhibitions, promotions, or starring roles in movies weren't the way to cope with his declining fame. In 1940 he decided to return to Columbus with his family—including another baby daughter, Beverly. He reenrolled at Ohio State to finish his studies and earn his college degree. While a student, he accepted a position as an assistant coach with the Ohio State track team.

Back in Columbus, Jesse found that he still could not concentrate on the courses required for graduation. The death of his father from a heart attack saddened him. After his first term, Jesse was expelled from Ohio State for low grades but was allowed to return for the next term and try once more. Through the next three academic quarters, Jesse struggled with his classwork. Finally, in December 1941, he left The Ohio State University for good, unable to reach the 1.5 grade point average needed to graduate.

That month was an important turning point for Jesse Owens and for the rest of the world. On December 7, 1941, Japan bombed the U.S. air and naval base at Pearl Harbor in Hawaii. The United States was suddenly at war with Japan and Germany.

During World War II, Jesse was hired to encourage African Americans to stay physically fit.

Chapter **SEVEN**

THE WORLD'S
FASTEST
MANAGER

FOR **E**UROPE, **WORLD WAR** II **HAD BEGUN IN S**EPTEMBER
1939, when German armies invaded Poland. In the
spring of 1940, Germany conquered France, Belgium,
and the Netherlands. Japan, Hitler's ally in Asia, invaded
China, Southeast Asia, and the Philippines. The 1940
Tokyo Olympic Games had been canceled before the
start of the war, and the Games scheduled for London
in 1944 would not take place either. By 1942, the entire
world seemed to be at war.

The United States officially entered the war on
December 8, 1941, the day after the attack on Pearl
Harbor. Because he was the head of a family, Jesse
Owens would not be required to serve in the military.
But in January 1942, the Civilian Defense Office asked

him to help run a government fitness program. He gave speeches on fitness and health and helped start exercise programs in African-American communities throughout the country. While leading a fitness clinic in Detroit, Michigan, in the fall of 1942, Jesse learned of a job opportunity with the Ford Motor Company.

Ford and its competitors in the auto industry built much-needed war supplies, making tanks, planes, guns, ammunition, and spare parts to ship to U.S. forces overseas. The Ford factories were running night and day. To meet its production schedule, the company hired thousands of new laborers to work the extra shifts on the assembly lines. Many of these workers were African-Americans who had moved to Detroit from other cities in the Midwest and from the South. As a personnel manager with Ford, Jesse would help oversee black workers at the company's various plants. He would check out job applicants, fire workers when necessary, and try to resolve disputes or problems between the workers and management.

The job was not easy, as workers and managers at Ford did not always get along. Although the workers were well paid, the boredom of their jobs on an assembly line and the strict rules enforced by their supervisors caused stress, fatigue, and dissatisfaction. During the mid-1930s, a union known as the United Auto Workers (UAW) had been established in Michigan to organize auto assembly-plant workers. At the beginning, Ford's managers had denied the union's right to exist,

Jesse never really felt comfortable at a desk job. He preferred to be active and to travel.

and the dispute had nearly led to open warfare in the company's plants. In the following years, the union fought hard to gain better working conditions, sick pay, and pensions for the company's workers.

Jesse's strongest qualification for his new job was his easygoing and polite manner. He managed to get along with most people he met, a trait that eased the sometimes bitter exchanges between workers and supervisors. Four months after the job began, Jesse was promoted to director of Negro personnel at Ford's River Rouge plant. The company also asked him to serve as a spokesperson for the community of black Ford workers who lived in and around Detroit.

In 1945, Henry Ford II took over as president of the company after his grandfather, Henry Ford, retired. Determined to change Ford's poor public image as an antilabor company, the new president fired many managers and personnel directors. As part of this effort, the company offered Jesse a reassignment to a lesser job in October 1945. Instead of accepting the change, however, Jesse turned it down. In turn, the company fired him.

To some of his friends, Jesse seemed almost happy to leave his job at Ford. In fact, he wasn't very well suited for a big corporation like the Ford Motor Company. He disliked the stress of a day-to-day management job. A restless and sometimes impatient person, he also found it hard to concentrate for long periods of time on the same task. Instead, he loved to travel and to divide his time among many different projects at once. He also preferred working alone, in front of an audience of spectators or listeners, where

Jesse urged parents to have their children vaccinated against polio.

he depended only on his own ability and enthusiasm to carry him through.

World War II ended in 1945 with the defeat of Germany and then Japan. Soon after, Jesse was traveling again with exhibition teams. He appeared with the Harlem Globetrotters, popular basketball clowns who performed stunts and jokes in front of large crowds. He also appeared with a baseball team called the Cincinnati Crescents. At the games, Jesse signed autographs and gave talks to the fans about his Olympic feats. He still entertained audiences with his running exhibitions, and often he nearly equaled his world-record times over short distances.

Jesse agreed to hundreds of exhibitions, speeches, fundraising appearances, and other public events. He often spent only a single night or even just a few hours in one place. The busy schedule was difficult for his wife and growing daughters. For weeks at a time, Jesse was away from home. Ruth Owens had to do her best to guide her three girls through childhood and school. In 1949 Jesse decided to move from Detroit to Chicago, a decision that, for his family, meant leaving behind friends, schools, and a home. Gloria, Jesse's eldest daughter, decided to remain with family friends in Detroit while finishing her last year of high school.

In Chicago, Jesse found that his fame as an Olympic gold medalist opened some important doors. Many different companies hired him to help promote their

Jesse worked with youth at the South Side Boys Club. Here, Jesse works with heavyweight boxing champion James T. Braddock.

products. He started his own public relations business and also spent time with charity groups such as the South Side Boys Club. He appeared on radio programs and worked as a master of ceremonies at banquets, meetings, and sporting events. He also began writing a regular column for the *Chicago Defender,* a newspaper that served the city's African-American community. The bitter memories of the late 1930s, when he had lost his amateur standing and failed at several business ventures, began to fade. He no longer needed to take part in small-town exhibition races or humiliating stunts.

The issues important to African-Americans—education, job opportunity, and justice—also held Jesse Owens's attention. In the 1950s, as he became a respected and prominent member of Chicago society, he found that many people, both black and white, were asking his opinion on these issues.

Jesse had already suffered his share of racial discrimination. He had seen outright racism as a young
track athlete in high school and college. Just after his
victories at the Olympic Games, he found that his
fame and gold medals still opened no doors to a
steady, good-paying job. But throughout his life, Jesse
believed strongly in self-reliance and in working
within the system, flawed as it sometimes could be.
All of his speeches included an important message:
people in the United States, regardless of their color
or background, could achieve their dreams through
hard work and perseverance.

Jesse had strong opinions, and both African-Americans and whites were interested in what he had to say.

Politicians and business leaders liked this positive message. After all, it reflected well on the society they had made and were leading. Jesse remained in high demand for political campaigns, and in 1952 he publicly supported the Republican candidate for governor of Illinois. This support, in turn, earned him rewards in the form of political appointments. In the next year, he won a position as secretary (head) of the Illinois State Athletic Commission. In this job, he traveled all over the state to supervise boxing matches. In 1955 Jesse was named the director of the new Illinois Youth Commission. This agency set up recreational programs and organized athletic events for juvenile delinquents throughout the state.

Jesse also found himself in demand by the United States government as a goodwill ambassador. After World War II had ended, the government of the United States was engaged in the "Cold War" with the Soviet Union. American leaders believed that democracy and a free-market economic system must win out over the Soviet Communist system—not necessarily by fighting, but by setting forth good examples, among other tactics.

In 1955, as part of this cold war effort, the United States Department of State asked Jesse to embark on a goodwill tour of Asia. He traveled to India, the Philippines, and Malaya to give talks, lead running clinics, and promote the economic and political freedoms of his home country. In 1956 he attended the Summer

Olympic Games in Melbourne, Australia, as a personal representative of U.S. President Dwight Eisenhower.

In Melbourne, as everywhere else, Jesse Owens was greeted warmly by politicians and fans. He also witnessed athletes running as fast, or faster, than he had ever run. By the late 1950s, track athletes were training longer and had the support of larger coaching staffs. They ran on dry, smooth surfaces and had the use of starting blocks. In the 1956 Olympics, they also had the entire summer to train because the Games took place during the U.S. winter months, when it was summer in Australia. That year's U.S. Olympic track team won most of the running and relay events. Members of the team also took home gold medals in the shot put, the discus throw, the pole vault, the hammer throw, the high jump, and the decathlon. In each of these events, the gold medalists set new Olympic records.

The star American sprinter that year was Bobby Morrow, who had come closer than anyone else to breaking Jesse's record in the 100-yard dash. Jesse was stunned to discover how much he cared about owning the record. "My 100-yard dash mark seemed connected to all kinds of other things—I didn't know what exactly—and if this boy wiped [it] from the books, he'd wipe them all away somehow."

As Jesse watched from the broadcasters' booth, Bobby Morrow took gold medals in both the 100-meter and 200-meter sprints. He was the first athlete to accomplish this feat since Jesse had done it twenty years earlier. Morrow's time in the 200-meter dash was 20.6 seconds, one-tenth of a second faster than Jesse's Berlin record of 20.7 seconds. Morrow also anchored the team that won the 400-meter relay race in the world-record time of 39.5 seconds, three-tenths of a second faster than the 1936 squad.

Jesse Owens went home to Chicago, thrilled at the victory of the U.S. track squad but disappointed about the end of his reign as the World's Fastest Human. After Melbourne, only one of his Olympic records remained: the mark of 26 feet, 5¼ inches he had set in the broad jump. Owens still held the world record as well: 26 feet, 8¾ inches. Both of these records stood until the summer of 1960. While qualifying for the Olympic team, Ralph Boston jumped an official mark of 26 feet, 11¼ inches. During the 1960 Summer Olympic Games held in Rome, Italy, Boston also set a new Olympic record with a broad jump of 26 feet, 7¾ inches.

The world records and the Olympic records set by Jesse Owens (that had lasted more than twenty years) had fallen, but Jesse was still a hero in Chicago. He was in great demand as a speaker, publicist, and community organizer, and his many different executive positions allowed him as much traveling and public speaking as he could stand. In 1960 he joined Richard M. Nixon's Republican presidential campaign against Democrat John F. Kennedy. But with the help of a

Jesse met with Richard Nixon (then Vice President) to support a fellow Republican.

very narrow victory in Chicago and in Illinois, Kennedy prevailed in that fall's election.

The community that admired, praised, and rewarded Jesse Owens also held him up as a role model. He had to set a good example wherever he went; every day, crowds of people were carefully watching and listening to him. Jesse thrived on all the attention, but he also found it intrusive. "There are many times now when I don't feel like doing something—signing autographs or speaking for an audience or having dinner with people I have never seen—but the public is not interested in explanations. You got to smile. You must. . . . If you are ordinary then the public can no longer look up to you."

Jesse found out the harsh truth of this statement in the 1960s. He was in his fifties and living well. But then current events and personal problems began to catch up with him. He soon looked all too human to the public.

Jesse had always been careless with money. Although he had quickly earned a high income in the years after the 1936 Olympics, he had spent it just as quickly. He had been a failure as a businessman. Several times he found that people whom he had trusted had taken advantage of him. In the mid-1960s, Jesse Owens found himself in trouble with the IRS again. Investigators working for the IRS discovered that Jesse had not filed any tax returns for several years in the late 1950s and early 1960s. Portions of his salaries from the Illinois State Athletic Commission and a public relations firm had been withheld for payment to the IRS, but Jesse had not paid taxes on the money he had made for product endorsements, speaking appearances, and other work. He was charged with income tax evasion in November 1965 and brought to a federal court for trial.

Jesse admitted that he had not filed the returns, but he also offered the court an explanation: he had been too busy traveling, meeting, and speaking. The court found him guilty of failing to pay nearly $70,000 in taxes and, in February 1966, fined him an additional $3,000. Because Jesse was a model citizen, he avoided serving time in prison. "It would be a travesty," said

Judge J. Sam Perry, "if I, under these circumstances, exercise my discretion improperly or excessively here against a good citizen for one mistake." But once again, Jesse faced a financial crisis. He owed more than $100,000 to the government and to the lawyers who had defended him in the case.

Somehow, he would have to make up the debt. For Jesse, it was almost like starting over again. This time, however, he found that being a role model and a good example can backfire. Since the public had such great expectations of him, many of his friends and supporters felt let down. Politicians stopped calling, and charity groups no longer wanted his services. His public relations business failed. "But I still had my friends," he later wrote. "I had them for about four hours after the first story hit the Chicago papers." As a famous man in his fifties, he might have hoped he could slow down and enjoy his success. Instead, he was entering one of the most troubled times of his life.

Protesting the war in Vietnam, this man confronts the National Guard.

Chapter **EIGHT**

CHANGING TIMES

LIKE EVERY OTHER SOCIAL LEADER OF THE **1960s,**
Jesse Owens found himself involved in bitter public
conflicts. The United States had entered a war in the
Asian nation of Vietnam, and millions of Americans,
especially college students and African-Americans,
were protesting against the war, against authority, and
against the "American way." In Chicago, Jesse saw
antiwar protesters battle police in the streets during
the 1968 Democratic National Convention. He also
witnessed protests staged by the Black Panthers, a
group dedicated to fighting racial inequality in the
United States.

Jesse strongly opposed the tactics used by these
protest movements, although he did not necessarily

oppose their goals. He saw himself, first and foremost, as a citizen of the United States and secondly as an African-American. He strongly believed in the American dream: the opportunity to succeed through work and patience regardless of one's race or circumstances. He didn't believe in protest marches or sit-down strikes. Although he hadn't served in World War II, Jesse didn't believe young men should avoid the draft or flee to Canada to protest the war in Vietnam, as many were doing.

Jesse found himself drawn into these controversies during 1968, an Olympic year. Black athletes were joining a growing movement to boycott the Games. The boycott, they believed, would serve to protest racism in the United States, U.S. involvement in the war in Vietnam, and the participation of an Olympic team from South Africa. At the time, South Africa followed racist laws and policies under a system called apartheid. As in 1936, the Olympic Games became a magnet for international political controversy and issues of social justice.

Jesse Owens spoke out publicly against the Olympic boycott movement. In newspaper columns and televised speeches, he said participating in the Olympic Games would be the best way for African-Americans to bridge the divide that separated whites and blacks. Although he supported the cause of social justice and equality, he believed the Olympic Games should be free of such problems and issues. The Games were an international, amateur athletic spectacle, he said, that should serve only as a showcase for the world's best athletes.

A few weeks before the Games were to begin in Mexico City, the International Olympic Committee decided to ban the South African team from competing, just as it had in 1964. Other African nations that had planned to boycott the Games changed their minds and decided to send their teams. The United States would also attend. Jesse Owens went as an official guest of the Mexican government. He worked for the U.S. Olympic Committee as a consultant and also worked as a radio announcer, as he had done at the Melbourne Games in 1956.

Perhaps the most astonishing athletic feat at the Mexico City Games took place during the long jump (formerly called the broad jump) competition. After barely qualifying for the finals, Bob Beamon of Long Island, New York, took his place for a run toward the long-jump pit. "He hurtled down the runway with maximum velocity," reported one writer. "He hit the takeoff board perfectly, had a perfect high arc and bunched his body perfectly in midair before straightening for a perfect landing. The crowd screamed in ecstatic disbelief." Beamon had jumped an amazing 29 feet, 2½ inches, smashing the world record by nearly two feet.

Beamon's long jump was the most impressive achievement of the U.S. Olympic track team that year. The

Medal winners Tommie Smith, center, *and John Carlos,* right, *give the Black Power salute during the 1968 Olympic awards ceremony.*

United States also won gold medals in the pole vault, the decathlon, the shot put, the high jump, two relays, and the 100-, 200-, and 400-meter races. But the protest movement was not forgotten by the athletes from the United States. After receiving their gold and bronze medals for the 200-meter dash, Tommie Smith and John Carlos bowed their heads and raised black-gloved fists toward the sky as a protest against racism, while the national anthem played. "The fact is the fight for right among blacks is bigger than the winning of any one event in sports," said Smith afterward. "I used victory as a means to an end, which will be reached when blacks have reached equal status in society. . . ."

The protest caused a sensation all over the world. The International Olympic Committee was determined to punish Smith and Carlos for their actions on the stand. That night, Jesse met with the two sprinters, as well as several other black members of the team, to address the situation. Jesse tried to persuade Smith and Carlos to apologize, but the meeting turned angry and bitter. To Smith and Carlos, Jesse's experiences in Hitler's Berlin had little or no connection to

Jesse asked John Carlos to publicly apologize for his Black Power salute.

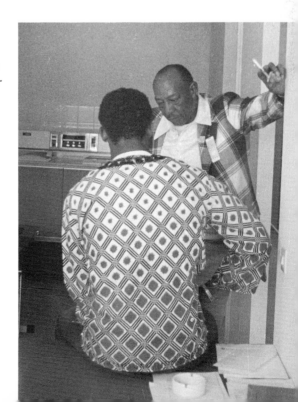

conditions in the United States of the 1960s. The two sprinters would not apologize. They were suspended from the team the following day.

Angered by the protest of Smith and Carlos, Jesse was inspired to begin work on an autobiographical book. He hired a writer named Paul Niemark as a collaborator. By the spring of 1970, the book was ready. Using memories of his own boyhood and his experiences as an African-American athlete, Jesse revealed his thoughts on race problems in the United States, on antiwar protesters, and on the actions of Tommie Smith and John Carlos. Jesse called his book *Blackthink: My Life as Black Man and White Man.*

Jesse made it plain in the book that he still believed in the American dream. He claimed that blacks in America were even better off than he had been in the 1930s as a college student. If blacks still felt the pain of discrimination and failure, he believed, they had to look inward for the causes. If they wanted to improve their lot, he insisted, they must simply work harder. He saved his sharpest words for militants, protesters, and draft dodgers who, he believed, simply could not appreciate the genuine economic opportunity they enjoyed in the United States—the only opportunity, in the end, that really mattered. "Sometimes they'll talk with you," he wrote about his militant black opponents. "But in the background is the gun and the knife, the riot and the revolution. . . . Even if the militants were right about every single thing they advocate, the means they're using and threatening to use to win their ends would make it all worthless."

Jesse's message set off angry criticism among many in the African-American community who believed he had lost touch with current events and problems in the United States. The racism he had fought by his example in Germany was the racism of a different time and a different nation. Jesse had become a successful, comfortable, and conservative figure—one writer called him "a professional good example." His fame had sheltered him from the racism African-Americans

Jesse didn't agree with the methods of many civil rights groups in the 1960s. This Black Panther office was the scene of a gun battle between local police and Black Panther members.

still suffered in schools, factories, stores, offices, and in the streets.

The criticism and controversy surrounding the book gave Jesse Owens second thoughts about *Blackthink*. Soon after the book appeared, he and Niemark began work on another project, called *I Have Changed*. In this new book, Jesse eased the sharp criticism he had expressed in *Blackthink*. As in his later books, he used his own experiences on the running track and at the Olympic Games to spin yarns that carried an important point. "I'd always been able to get off a fraction of an instant before the other runners," he wrote, ". . . not by listening for the gun as they did, but by watching the gunman's eyes. You can almost always tell from a man's eyes what he's going to do next. Too bad it takes most of us a lifetime to look into our own."

In *I Have Changed*, Jesse wrote in detail about his struggles, his problems, and his own shortcomings as a businessman and father. He acknowledged that blacks in the United States still faced difficult barriers and admitted that in many ways his country was deeply troubled. But he still insisted that men and women of any color and nationality could succeed in a country that offered them more opportunity than any other.

At the end of *I Have Changed*, Jesse admitted that his best days were behind him. He looked back over his life with honesty, seeing the bad as well as the good, the defeats as well as the victories. Above all, he

Jesse Owens, right, *is greeted by officials as he arrives in Germany for the Munich Olympic Games in 1972.*

wanted to keep moving, as fast as he possibly could. "I know I'll drop in my tracks someday," he wrote. "And I won't really mind if it comes sooner than it should, as long as I'm making tracks when I drop."

Jesse's optimism and positive message certainly brought him support and opportunity from businesses throughout the country. He signed or renewed contracts with several large corporations for promotional appearances and traveled widely to deliver speeches on the themes he had discussed in his books. He was still in demand as a supporter of Republican candidates for political office and spent much of his time promoting the efforts of the U.S. Olympic team. In 1972 Jesse returned to Germany to witness the first Olympics held there since 1936. The 1972 Games, held in the West German city of Munich, turned tragic when a Palestinian terrorist organization took a group of Israeli athletes hostage. During a bloody shoot-out with German police, the terrorists killed eleven of their hostages.

Another incident was nearly forgotten in the shadow of the attack on the Israeli team. This time, two 400-meter medalists, Vincent Matthews and Wayne Collett, turned their backs to the American flag during the national anthem. Jesse was again called on to meet with the protesting athletes and try to get them to apologize for their actions, but they would not.

Jesse Owens may have felt as if he was losing touch with young people and with African-American athletes. But he still was a highly respected figure who earned warm praise nearly everywhere he went. In 1972, The Ohio State University awarded him an honorary degree as a doctor of athletic arts. Two years later, the NCAA gave him the Theodore Roosevelt Award for achievements he made after leaving amateur athletics. The Track and Field Hall of Fame voted him a member in the same year. In 1976 President Gerald Ford presented him with the Medal of Freedom, the highest civilian honor given by the U.S. government.

Jesse still traveled from place to place giving speeches, presenting awards, and appearing at athletic events. His opinions on modern athletics, amateurism, and the Olympic Games still mattered to fans as well as to powerful officials. He found himself drawn into yet another Olympic controversy in 1979, when President Jimmy Carter called for the United States to boycott the 1980 Summer Games, scheduled to take place in the Soviet capital of Moscow. Carter and others wanted the boycott to serve as a protest of the Soviet invasion of Afghanistan. At first, Jesse supported the boycott movement. Later, however, he changed his mind. The Olympics, he believed, should always stand above the concerns of political and military rivalry between nations. He announced his support for a plan that would have the athletes compete as individuals and not as part of an official team. As it turned out, the boycott occurred, and no U.S. athletes competed in Moscow.

By late 1979, Jesse found himself fatigued and suffering from a terrible cough. For many years, he had been a heavy cigarette smoker and the deadly habit had finally caught up with him. He returned to Chicago and checked himself into a hospital, where he learned that he had lung cancer. After hearing the news, he returned to the home he and Ruth had purchased in Scottsdale, Arizona. For several months, he struggled through chemotherapy treatments. But the illness was far advanced. On March 31, 1980, Jesse Owens passed away in Tucson, Arizona. A few days later, his funeral took place in Chicago.

This bronze statue stands in the Jesse Owens Memorial Park in Oakville, Alabama.

Many different cities and organizations found ways to honor Jesse Owens after he died. The Ohio State University, where Jesse had starred but not graduated, built a new facility for its track team and named it the Jesse Owens Track. The school also built the Jesse Owens Memorial Plaza. The Jesse Owens Memorial Foundation provided athletic scholarships to young athletes, and a Jesse Owens Invitational track meet started in New York. In East Berlin, Germany, a street leading to the Olympic Stadium was named after the star of the 1936 Olympics. A stone monument was also raised in Oakville, Alabama—Jesse's birthplace.

During the opening ceremonies of the 1984 Olympics in Los Angeles, Gina Hemphill carried the Olympic torch once around the running track in memory of her grandfather, Jesse Owens. This may have been the most significant memorial service that was ever performed for Jesse Owens. It was on the running track, after all, that Jesse had earned his fame and reached one of the high points of his athletic career and his life. And it was for his 10.3-second, 100-meter dash past the eyes of a dictator and for his nation that Jesse Owens will always be remembered.

SOURCES

12   William J. Baker, *Jesse Owens: An American Life* (New York: The Free Press, 1986), 11.

15–16   Jesse Owens and Paul Neimark, *Jesse: The Man who Outran Hitler* (Plainfield, N.J.: Logos International, 1978) 28.

17   Tony Gentry, *Jesse Owens: Champion Athlete*, Black Americans of Achievement series (New York: Chelsea House Publishers, 1990), 28.

18–19   Richard D. Mandell, *The Nazi Olympics* (New York: The Macmillan Company, 1971), 227.

20   Owens, Niemark, *Jesse*, 47.

20   Gentry, 55.

26   Baker, 30.

33–34   Bill Libby, *Stars of the Olympics* (New York: Hawthorn Books, Inc., 1975), 67.

35   *Jesse Owens*, The Black Americans of Achievement/ Video Collection II. Schlessinger Video Productions, 1994.

40   Mandell, 75.

41–42   Owens, Niemark, *Jesse*, 61.

42   Ibid., 78.

48   Albert Speer, *Inside the Third Reich* (New York: The Macmillan Company, 1982), 73.

48   Gentry, 13.

51   Baker, 93.

54   Owens, Niemark, *Jesse*, 62.

55   Gentry, 68.

57   Baker, 104.

59   Speer, 73.

63   Libby, 68.

72   Gentry, 85.

75   Jesse Owens, with Paul Niemark, *Blackthink: My Life as Black Man and White Man* (New York: Pocket Books, 1971), 40.

87   Owens, Niemark, *Jesse* 137–38.

89	Baker, 183.
90–91	Ibid., 204.
91	Jesse Owens, with Paul Niemark, *I Have Changed*, (New York: William Morrow, 1972), 48.
95	Kieran, 435.
96–97	Libby, 132.
98–99	Owens, Niemark, *Blackthink*, 90.
99	William O. Johnson, *All That Glitters Is Not Gold* (New York: G. P. Putnam's Sons, 1972), 51.
100	Owens, Niemark, *I Have Changed*, 31.
101	Ibid., 152.

BIBLIOGRAPHY

Baker, William J. *Jesse Owens: An American Life.* New York: The Free Press, 1986.

Gentry, Tony. *Jesse Owens: Champion Athlete.* New York: Chelsea House Publishers, 1990.

Jesse Owens. The Black Americans of Achievement/Video Collection II. Schlessinger Video Productions, 1994.

Johnson, William O. *All That Glitters Is Not Gold.* New York: G. P. Putnam's Sons, 1972.

Kieran, John, and Arthur Daley. *The Story of the Olympic Games.* Philadelphia: J. B. Lippincott, 1973.

Libby, Bill. *Stars of the Olympics.* New York: Hawthorn Books, Inc., 1975.

Mandell, Richard D. *The Nazi Olympics.* New York: The Macmillan Company, 1971.

Olympia: Festival of the People. Produced and directed by Leni Riefenstahl. Sandy Hook, Connecticut: Video Yesteryear, 1980.

Owens, Jesse, with Paul Niemark. *Blackthink: My Life as Black Man and White Man.* New York: Pocket Books, 1971.

Owens, Jesse, with Paul Niemark. *I Have Changed.* New York: William Morrow, 1972.

Owens, Jesse, and Paul Neimark. *Jesse: The Man who Outran Hitler.* Plainfield, N.J.: Logos International, 1978.

Sanford, William R., and Carl R. Green. *Jesse Owens.* Sports Immortals series. New York: Crestwood House, 1992.

INDEX

OTHER TITLES IN LERNER'S BIOGRAPHY® SERIES:

Arthur Ashe
Christopher Reeve
Legends of Dracula
Louisa May Alcott
Madeleine Albright
Maya Angelou

Mother Teresa
Nelson Mandela
Princess Diana
Rosie O'Donnell
Women in Space

ABOUT THE AUTHOR

Tom Streissguth was born in Washington, D.C., and grew up in Minneapolis. He has written more than 30 books for young people, including *Writer of the Plains: A Story about Willa Cather, Mary Cassatt: Portrait of an American Impressionist, Say it with Music: A Story about Irving Berlin,* and *Legends of Dracula.* Tom lives with his family in Florida.

PHOTO ACKNOWLEDGMENTS

Library of Congress, 2, 55; The Ohio State University Archives, 6, 7, 19, 24, 27, 28, 30, 36, 54, 58, 63, 84, 85; © Archive Photos, 8; Jesse Owens Memorial Park Board, 10, 104; Corbis-Bettmann, 13; National Archives, 14; The Cleveland Press Collection, 15, 21; Cleveland Public Library Photograph Collection, 17, 43, 65, 72, 73; Corbis-Bettmann Archives/Cleveland Public Library, 33, 78, 82; UPI/ Corbis-Bettmann, 44, 47, 52, 60, 62, 68, 71, 74, 81, 89, 92, 96, 99, 101; AP/Wide World Photos, 97.

Front Cover: UPI/Corbis-Bettmann
Back Cover: The Ohio State University Archives